SEA LIONS

THE SEA MAMMAL DISCOVERY LIBRARY

Sarah Palmer

Rourke Enterprises, Inc.
Vero Beach, Florida 32964

Library of Congress Cataloging-in-Publication Data

Palmer, Sarah, 1955-
  Sea lions.

  (The Sea mammal discovery library)
  Includes index.
  Summary: Describes the appearance, species,
and behavior of sea lions.
  1. Sea lions—Juvenile literature. [1. Sea lions]
I. Title.
II. Series: Palmer, Sarah, 1955-
Sea mammal discovery library.
QL737.P63P34   1989   599.74'6   88-26431
ISBN 0-86592-362-0

TABLE OF CONTENTS

SEA LIONS

Sea lions are sometimes called "eared seals." Unlike true seals, they have external ears that can be seen clearly. There are five **species** of sea lions. Two species live in the northern **hemisphere** and three in the southern hemisphere. The two kinds of northern sea lions are the Californian (*Zalophus californianus*) and the Steller (*Eumetopias jubatus*). Southern sea lions can be found in Australia, New Zealand, and South America.

Sea lions' ears can easily be seen

HOW THEY LOOK

Sea lions hold their heads high on long, strong necks. Their skins are shades of brown. Some are yellowish tan, and others are quite dark. Very young sea lions are dark brown. When their skins are wet, sea lions look almost black. Sea lions have large, webbed **flippers**. On land, sea lions fold their back flippers forward underneath their bodies and use their front flippers for support.

Sea lions' skins vary from light to dark brown

CALIFORNIAN AND STELLER SEA LIONS

Californian and Steller sea lions are the only sea lions that live in U.S. waters. Both kinds can be seen along the coasts of California and Oregon. Steller sea lions are the largest of all the eared seals. Males often weigh over a ton (2,000 lbs.) and are three times as big as their Californian cousins. Male sea lions are always much bigger than female ones. Most zoos and marine parks have Californian sea lions.

Steller sea lions are the largest eared seals

WHERE THEY LIVE

Steller sea lions are found near Alaska in the Pribilof Islands and the Aleutian Islands. They also live along the Alaskan and Californian coastline and on islands in the Sea of Okhotsk, to the east of the U.S.S.R. Californian sea lions can be found along the Pacific Coast from Canada to Mexico. One **subspecies** of Californian sea lions lives farther south in the Galapagos Islands.

A subspecies of Californian sea lions lives in the Galapagos Islands

A mother sea lion and her pup walk proudly to the ocean

This male sea lion is quite big!

WHAT THEY EAT

Sea lions eat all kinds of fish, depending on what is most plentiful. Scientists have found that sea lions eat hake (similar to cod), anchovies, salmon, and even small sharks. Octopus, squid, and shellfish have also been found in the stomachs of dead sea lions. Large groups of sea lions often gather to feed on **schools** of fish or squid. Southern sea lions sometimes eat penguins also.

Groups of sea lions gather to feed on schools of fish

LIVING IN THE OCEAN

Sea lions use their strong front flippers to propel themselves through the water. Although not as fast as dolphins or whales, sea lions are strong swimmers. In experiments, scientists have watched sea lions swim as fast as 22 M.P.H. Sea lions often make deep dives to the ocean floor for food. It is not certain how deep they can dive. Scientists have trained some to dive over 800 feet below the water.

Sea lions are very graceful swimmers

THEIR BODIES

Under their skin, sea lions have a thick layer of fat called **blubber**. This keeps them warm in the cold oceans. If the water is very cold, they sometimes huddle together for extra warmth. In summer, sea lions can find the sun too warm as they bask on the rocky shores. They position their bodies in a special way to keep cool. If they become very hot, sea lions jump into the cold ocean to cool off.

A sea lion basks in the sun as she suckles her pup

BABY SEA LIONS

In the Californian Channel Islands, sea lion **pups** are born in late May and June each year. Each mother sea lion has just one pup. After about two weeks, the pup has its first swimming lesson. It is nervous in the water and swims awkwardly. By the time it is six weeks old, though, it swims well and can fully control its breathing and movement.

A Californian sea lion pup

THE SEA LION FAMILY

Female sea lions take care of their pups for one year after they are born. They teach them to swim and to catch food. The male sea lions do not stay with the mothers and pups. After the **breeding season** each year, the adult males lead the sea lions' **migration**. The whole population moves to a different place. The female sea lions and their young follow about a month later.

GLOSSARY

blubber (BLUH ber) — a thick layer of fat under the skin of a sea mammal

breeding season (BREED ing SEE zun) — the time of year when animals mate

flippers (FLI purz) — broad, flat limbs that help a seal to swim

hemisphere (HEM is feer) — one half of the world

migration (mi GRAY shun) — movement from one place to another, usually at the same time each year

pups (PUP s) — baby sea lions

schools (SKOOLZ) — groups of whales, dolphins, or fish

species (SPEE seez) — a scientific term meaning kind or type

subspecies (SUB SPEE seez) — a scientific term meaning a group within a species

INDEX